THE
DISTANT
SIREN

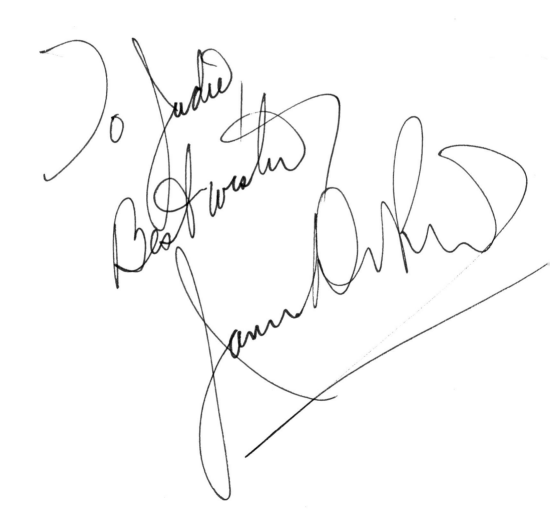

To Judie
Best of wishes

JAMES DEPREIST

THE
DISTANT
SIREN

Foreword by Maya Angelou

WILLAMETTE UNIVERSITY PRESS
SALEM, OREGON
1989

THE DISTANT SIREN
Poems by James DePreist
Copyright © 1989 by James DePreist

Willamette University Press
Office of News & Publications
Willamette University
900 State Street
Salem, OR 97301

International Standard Book Number 0-9623976-0-1 8.00
Library of Congress Catalog Card Number 89-85361

196DEV889.5MYTP

For Ginette

There is obviously poetry in the orchestral conducting of James DePreist and audible musicality in the poetry of James DePreist. His second collection of poetry has the tautness of a perfectly pitched viola and much of its resonance.

DePreist's eye of poesy leads him into sanctums which might appear at first glance unexciting, but he enters and finds depths and shades and melodies and promise.

> "AUGUST
>   jealous of September's prize
>   drips its resentment
>   like a
>   too-full sponge
>   exacting tolls bitter
>   and exorbitant
>   for the annual right of passage home"

There is Haiku-like brevity in many of the poems and it is obvious that the poet is capable of condensing lifetimes and relationships into powerful images. His four desolate, but non-pitying lines

> "IN LONELINESS LAMENTED
>   those absent loves
>   in surfeit
>   spurned"

are perfect in their density and irreducible language.

Here the cosmos is filled with delusion and despair. Yet, strangely the poems are testament of faith.

DePreist, as poet conductor, directs the reader away from cynicism. The reader is encouraged to look softly toward the closing of a circle, and to be unafraid of its center.

The title poem reveals to the reader the potent threat of the external influences. Yet, we are assured that love protects all, and even redeems all.

> "MY GRANDMOTHER BROUGHT
> the distant siren's tension among
> the peace of our unaffected home
> with
> words that spoke the compass of
> her soul and never let us, untouched,
> hear
> a
> siren's song
> again.
> 'Poor somebody,' she said."

We are made rich by this contribution.

Maya Angelou
July 1989

THE
DISTANT
SIREN

Dıalectic's pendulum

    in antithesis detained

makes more

        of a thesis

than

    I

      thought

IN LONELINESS LAMENTED
those absent loves
in surfeit
spurned

THE CHARACTERLESS
                characters,
so perfectly processed
                endanger
uniquely spilled ribbons
of
    legible
            thought

THE SOFT, SILENT, FLUID SYMBOL
for a not-so-sovereign state of change
unfurls in the breeze of battle
a power-weave of
innocent threads for
souls of fortune
to rally
        'round

THE MECHANISM'S INTERNAL LOGIC
smoothly suits the outer chaos.
    Scene shifts
        flow
in the
      three-dimensional
            traffic
              of casts
confused, confident, consonant, colliding.
              A hand
too unseen choreographs
this real play that tempts tamperers
with mirrored lures

VULNERABILITY'S
long loved stumble
in a much admired
march of strength
yields a binding absence
we yearn to fill—
attached—
       forever

DEATH
is
the tunnel
at
the end
of our
light

ANOTHER LOANED DAY
    dims towards dusk;
spent splendor
           blazing its balance
before night wipes clean
the canvas
      for
        the brush of morning

GROUNDED ENOUGH
to fly
 without
  fear

A SWEET

        soft

           silence

hugs

    this

      moment

          eternal

REHEARSED, RELIC-LADEN
remembrance enshrining ritual
revisited riches
reaching from revered past
retuning the consonance of our faith
to remind with repetition
of the reason
                    for
                         renewal

TWENTY-FOUR TREES
frame the river with bough-shaped
      slices of view in
   sky light filtered through
leaf-lace
this the domain of tree-top travelers
and lapping tides
where noiselessly
clouds collide in infinity's blue
this textured
        haste repellent
           peace
seduces

FLEETINGLY,
despite the mist of circumstance
I seem to apprehend
an outline of context—
a suggestion of texture and density of
cast shadows—dispassionately real
yet evanescent—

        an interim view
from future's hindsight
informing the present

           of

            a

              work

                in progress

A LANDSCAPE
newly bathed in ambiguous hues
of nuanced shadow
mocks the certitude
of yesterday when
fading fear seemed to impel
a vault beyond habit

THE STRANGENESS SURROUNDS AND CLOTHES
impulse in unease
a fair cost for regretted ruptures
now bleeding pain
on the summer grass

THE
    gift
        of
           light
slips past the gloom-grey shield
    to save
        those
               running slightly off-balance
               in
               quicksand

SOME LEAVENING JUSTICE
would be in order—
    some relieving light;
       the scent of an answer
to symptom hope. Instead
    the thrice encrusted Why?
thickens
       to
        forest 'round its cul-de-sac
       in the dense and sullen foliage
        of despair

SOMEHOW WE CAN
never keep
the visions vivid
imperceptibly they
dance their glories
into shadow

WE ARE
　　　escapees all
pocketing history's change
　　　on the run

THIS MASSIVE SHOW OF FORCE
      impresses.
   Phalanx
    follows
       flurried
          phalanx—
Particles uncountable
        briefly clinging
to frozen life
     then
    taking root to deeply layer
the ground
    in
     white

MORE THAN ATTACHED—SYNONYMOUS
with this precious
    bubble
tenants in and of its
    fragile film
we are magnified and magnify
    beyond the zone of danger
the us and ours on temporary loan—
    essential ephemera whose accustomed
presence tempts us to ignore the
    vapor-thin transparency
    we think so firm

TENANTS OF TIME,
marvel and malaise
defy both
prolonging embrace and shunning;
duration destined
impeccable companions
we only contaminate
with
tampering

AUGUST
jealous of September's prize
drips its resentment
like a
too-full sponge
exacting tolls bitter
and exorbitant
for the annual right of passage
home

BRIDGES
        thrust
             past
                  mid-chasm
Offend the shared task,
      usurping another's traveled reach
                        toward
            center

Its luminous links
    dimming towards death,
the
    circle
        thins,
growing
       day
          by
            day
darker,
as filaments of memory
    spin off to hold, in gossamer grips,
the miracles still left—
arcing the ache
       where
          souls
            once
              were

AT AN EARLIER TIME

    it would have been scripted

        as   dreamed

destined

      delivered

             correlation

                 exact

now synchronous orbits

        unneeded

            spin elsewhere

with

    recurring proof

that

    here

       they are not

"SUCCINCTLY PUT,"
two words
too many

SUBLIME EXPECTATIONS—

    We had come to play Mozart

        in a church

            in June

                in the country.

Music transcendent

    had drawn us together—

a worship of wills in privileged communion—

all conspired to joyous sweet beauty

till

    we saw the atrocious echo of evil

a spectre too real that soon was beside us

the boots, the dog, the uniform of this Nazi

out for a stroll in this venue

                of peace

WE STRUT
the ramparts of our existence
landlords of

        a

          bubble

A
  linkage
      of lessons
         and
           final exams
that
  some
    seem
      to
       view
         as
          unsupervised
             recess

NIGHT FRIGHT
    flowing from a reservoir
of mysterious
            inquietude
simmers
      in the glare of
      street lights that give no warm
comfort
      but cast   instead
shadows
      cold
        on a cityscape
      sinister
          yet
            innocent

AN OBSCURED JUNCTION
suggests the point
where parallel fates
diverge,
when a destiny assumed,
escaped
      to
        less
           presumptive mirrors

MANIPULATED BY CIRCUMSTANCE
    in
    the shallows
        of reason
  we sing the silence—
    become
      the
        wind

WINNING

        oft

            wrests

     triumph trivial

          for

ultimate games

    are seldom

found

    on

        apparent

fields

   of

     play

P<small>AST</small>

    whispers

          transformed

now scream a message

I

  cannot

      hear

House shadows
    etched on sunned porch planks
    (four then, twelve now)
gulls
    above—
        practicing—
showing off really, their improvised tracings
that never collide
three-dimensional spatial counterpoint
    free, floating—
        flaunted fun

THIS UNMAPPED HERE
suffices

DANGLING
        within—keys to unmet wonders
permitting
                privileged
                        passage
                to
            our homes
            unknown
in the deepest unlit layer of
                        self

Unbid echoes of resignation
sigh
through now-new canyons
bathing mountains
in the
inevitable
sounds
of
parting

THEIR STYLE
    is seductive
but these are no more than
    glancing gestures;
      meteors deaf
        and politic
          that
            tangent
   the troubling
      circles
        of substance

Sleep

    eludes

        seeking

   dissolving   in   the glare

   of fatigued consciousness

      a reluctant partner

        for

insomnial

      dancing

More than mere
linguistic Lego
they should be symptoms of ideas;
thought armed with utterance
unfurled meanings
in the breeze
of
risk

BOTTOM-LINERS BEWARE:
there's
      another
set
of
books

WHEN SLEEP CONFIRMS OUR ABSENCE
the councils of night convene to script
            tomorrow
(laying out clothes for the coming day).
Awake,
            not privy to patterns in absentia
            plotted
            we presume
control,
            naively casting
                        coincidence
                                    as
                                        cause
and mistaking
            the gift of gliding for
                        powered
                                    flight

WE HAVEN'T A CLUE
    as to outcome;
coincident confluences—the luck of the draw
hunches, history, Hail Marys
                        and chutzpah
limp us through lifetimes.
But no one *knows;*
                not really
despite rantings and claims to be
        certitude's intimates
we're all labrynthian travelers
      mapless
          with faith

ONE LONGS FOR THE
    circle's neutral
        center
the bystander's disinterest.
But that surely can never be
    till death—
life's meantime has us trying
to cram in vain
hexagonal dreams
    into triangular reality

Is there room for you,
you ask—
there is more than room;
    the need to spill
with purpose,
        streams
              of
                  tender
                      ribboning time

No one
     knew
there were to be
     no minutes more
ever,
suddenly, on the heels of now
       came
          nothing

TIME ELAPSED

       crates the past

bundling

    our

       inventoried "are"

in the gathered minutiae

   of

   having been

ANTICIPATING USE
the energy,
meticulously stored,
seeps at each false call
and comes,
too often teased
            to rest
                    in the face
        of authentic summons
        —a force spent

THE CAMERA SENSED
what other lenses
once had seen
only to forget
in the flow of time
and flood of presence.
Lost focus regained
through the
frozen poignance
of one captured instant

WITHIN

    the

        embrace

            of

              distant

                  memory

crimson plumes persist,

   smile-scented

           random

              joyous

My grandmother brought

the distant siren's tension among
the peace of our unaffected home
with

words that spoke the compass of
her soul and never let us, untouched,

hear

a

siren's song

again.

"Poor somebody," she said.

TOMORROW
is
fully booked

COLOPHON

This edition of *The Distant Siren* has been designed and typeset by Susan Blettel, at Willamette University, Salem, Oregon. The cover is reproduced from hand marbled paper by Max Marbles, Salem. The paper is Mohawk Superfine and the type is Palatino. Printing is by Your Town Press, Salem, with color separations by Spectrum West, Portland. Linotronic type output by SalemType.

This book was prepared on a Macintosh IIcx computer with Aldus Pagemaker page layout program and Adobe fonts.

Two hundred and sixty copies have been bound in leather and marbled paper, and numbered and signed by the author.